INDIAN POTTERY

BY TONI ROLLER
OF
SANTA CLARA PUEBLO

Toni Roller

SANTA FE

front cover: picture of author, Toni Roller

Sunstone books may be purchased for educational, business, or sales promotional use. For information please write: Special Markets Department, Sunstone Press, P.O. Box 2321, Santa Fe, New Mexico 87504-2321.

FIRST EDITION

10 9 8 7 6 5 4 3 2

Library of Congress Cataloging in Publication Data:
Roller, Toni, 1935–
    Indian pottery / by Toni Roller of Santa Clara Pueblo.—1st ed.
       p. cm.
    Includes bibliographical references and index.
    ISBN: 0-86534-236-6 (pbk.)
       1. Pottery craft—New Mexico—Santa Clara Pueblo.   2. Roller, Toni,
1935–   .   3. Tewa pottery—New Mexico—Santa Clara Pueblo.   4. Indian
pottery-New Mexico—Santa Clara Pueblo.   I. Title.
TT919. 7. N62S267   1997
738.3' 089' 974—dc21   97-16532
                                              CIP

Published by SUNSTONE PRESS
           Post Office Box 2321
           Santa Fe, NM 87504-2321 / USA
           (505) 988-4418 / *orders only* (800) 243-5644
           FAX (505) 988-1025

CONTENTS

BACKGROUND ON PUEBLO INDIAN POTTERY

When early North American Indians first engaged in agriculture and banded together in communities, they recognized the need for containers to store their grain. These containers, made as early as 50 A.D., were woven baskets. About 700 A.D., the first Pueblo Indian experimented with clay; and pottery, fashioned after the original baskets, soon appeared in the Indian home. The early pottery was utilitarian and not considered art. The large containers stored dried materials; the smaller pieces, with concave bases for carrying on the head, were used to transport water and milk.

The opening of the Santa Fe Trail and the birth of railroads in the American Southwest introduced the Indian to European and American tableware. These wares replaced the traditional pottery. However, visitors to the area became intrigued by the Pueblo Pottery and wanted to take Indian curios back to their homes in the East. The Indians catered to this tourist trade, but turned out what one would term "junk ware."

Indian pottery making as an art form was reborn in the early 1900's with the revival of the Fiesta de Santa Fe and the First Annual Southwest Indian Fair.

Individual potters were not known by name until the late 1800's and did not begin signing their pieces until the 1920's.

After almost a century of being bundled together under the mass ethnic label of "Indian Art," certain artists have emerged as singular entities, expressing both their individualism and their Indian heritage.

Santa Clara Pueblo, located along the Rio Grande River, is the residence of more than 70 potters, many of them descendants of SaraFina Tafoya, a recognized artisan. SaraFina's mother and grandmother were Santa Clara Potters in the 1800's. The Pueblo's potters are known for their creativity, excellence of design, and quality and quantity of production. Santa Clara is also credited with the development of the black pottery, which is so popular today.

FORWARD

To have known Toni Roller's family and their increasing achievements for about twenty five years has been a privilege, an education, and a pleasure. A visit with this hospitable family is always a rewarding experience.

The outgoing Toni is both proud and serious about her Tewa Indian heritage and rightly so. Many centuries ago, when prehistoric wandering bands of Native Americans settled into agricultural communities, vessels became a necessity for the preparation and storage of food and mud lined baskets evolved into ceramic forms. Toni's specialty, black reduced fired pottery, first appeared at Santa Clara Pueblo between 1720 and 1800 AD having developed from a prehistoric Tewa plainware.

The Tafoya family credits SaraFina, Toni's grandmother, with being among the first potters to be known by name because of a fine reputation. Her children began signing their work and, when manufactured ceramics became available, Santa Clara pottery evolved from utilitarian pottery into an art form. Not until recent times were any male potters recognized.

As a daughter of Margaret Tafoya, Toni grew up absorbing the rudiments of traditional pottery making, but not until she married and the Rollers returned to live at the Pueblo, did she find the time and have the calling to carry on the family tradition. Many other responsibilities required her attention (seven children to mention a few), but her skills kept improving and she never lost her ambition to excel in her field. Today she competes with many Santa Clara pottery artists, some of whom are her relatives, and has earned numerous awards for her achievements.

A hard working lady, she is fortunate to have a supportive husband and family. Several of her children are now producing quality work. A studio near her home is a work place for all the Rollers, creating an excellent showcase for visitors and buyers to observe all the processes involved in making pottery from the raw clay to the finished product. The studio has been a social and financial success attracting tourists and collectors year round. Another innovation initiated by the Rollers is a Tafoya family show at the studio on the day before the S.W.A.I.A. Indian Market in Santa Fe every August when relatives may bring their work for show or sale. There is always good attendance at this event, pottery sells early, refreshments are served, friendships are made and renewed, and a happy relaxed atmosphere prevails.

Modern conveniences such as indoor plumbing for running water and materials such as manufactured paint brushes, instead of rabbit fur for applying slip, are used to ease some of the hard work, but it cannot be stressed enough that the Rollers always use traditional materials and methods by today's standards. They dig the Santa Clara clay and do the backbreaking task of washing and mixing it. Coiling, scraping, sanding, slipping, and stone polishing are all done by hand. Perhaps most important and requiring the most skill is the firing in an outdoor bonfire. For this they are financially compensated as well they should be. The easily available electric kilns are controllable and almost always insure a successful result, but a vessel fired in the traditional manner is risky and takes extraordinary expertise. It is a gamble, either destroying a vessel or resulting in a warm and glowing object of beauty deserving reward.

Toni is a spirited and enthusiastic person, demanding perfection in her work and is generously willing to share her knowledge. There are no "secrets" about her materials or methods. A trait much to be admired is her attitude toward her work: while making a commercial success of her pottery in today's competitive market, she has maintained her ancestral inheritance of respecting "Mother Clay."

—Mary Ellen Blair

INTRODUCTION

I am a daughter of Margaret Tafoya, the famous Indian potter of Santa Clara Pueblo in New Mexico. Santa Clara Pueblo is about one and one-half miles south of Espanola, New Mexico, on the Los Alamos highway.

I make the traditional black carved Santa Clara Indian pottery completely by hand using only materials from nature and fired in an outdoor fire. This black pottery and also some red is what Santa Clara Pueblo is really known for. People from all over the world have heard of Santa Clara Indian pottery. Collectors and traders from many places travel hundreds and even thousands of miles to come to Santa Clara or to an arts and crafts show where they can buy Santa Clara pottery.

I learned to make pottery by watching my mother, Margaret Tafoya and, of course, I think she was the best traditional Indian potter ever. Margaret Tafoya was a winner of The National Heritage Fellowship Award for the Arts in 1984. She is in her 90's now and is able to do only small pieces and only a few each year. Margaret learned to make pottery from her mother, or my grandmother, SaraFina Tafoya.

In those days my grandfather, Geronimo Tafoya, helped my grandmother, SaraFina, with her pottery. SaraFina was known for pottery having concave bases which were used for carrying liquids on the head.

I am sure my mother in her youth learned the fine points of how to make good pottery from her mother. This was long before she and my father were married. Tafoya was my mother's maiden name, but she and my father were in no way blood relations.

My father also helped my mother with as much of the hard pottery work as she would allow. Since he had not been physically able to help for years before he died, I, my sisters, and a brother would help my mother by doing the heavy and hard work such as digging the clay, bringing and cutting firing wood, hauling manure, and firing her pottery.

After our parents grew old, four of us sisters, myself, Shirley, Mary, Jennie, and a brother Leo, took turns staying with them twenty-four hours at a time. Then after my father died, my brother Wayne and my daughter Susan joined us and are taking their turns staying with my mother.

My mother Margaret Tafoya's pottery has become very valuable, especially now that she only makes a few pieces. My parents raised a large family of thirteen children and most of the family became very good potters so the fine work of Margaret is being carried on. My two sons, Cliff Roller, Jeff Roller, and a Daughter, Susan Roller Whittington are fine full-time potters. I also have two grandsons, Charles Lewis and Ryan Roller, who do some nice pottery part-time. So this makes four generations of potters at present. There were three known, but deceased, generations of potters before Margaret Tafoya, which makes my grandchildren seventh generation of all-time family potters, as far as is known. There is evidence that pottery may have been made, in this lineage, hundreds of years before these seven generations.

My sisters who are doing pottery are, Jennie Trammel, Lu Ann Tafoya, Mary Archuleta, and Shirley Tafoya. My oldest sister, Virginia Ebelacker, does not make pottery any more because of physical health problems.

I began to work seriously with my pottery during 1968, when I made my first sale, and I also had my first art show that year.

I did not enter my work for judging in shows until 1973 when I started receiving awards and since then, I am thankful for having done well with awards each year.

I thank God for my abilities and my mother for my learning experiences. I do the traditional Indian shapes, designs, and also some of my own contemporary styles.

I sell most of my pottery at my own Studio and Gallery which we opened in 1986. It is next to my home in Santa Clara Pueblo and is wheelchair accessible. We call it "Green Leaves" Studio which is my Indian name. Most of my pottery has gone to private collectors all around the United States, Canada, West Germany, Japan, England, Denmark, Australia, The Vatican in Italy, and U. S. President Clinton. Not many of my pieces go to arts and crafts shops or galleries because I do not sell wholesale.

Some museums that have my pottery are: The Albuquerque Museum, Albuquerque, New Mexico; The Museum of New Mexico, Santa Fe, New Mexico; The Indian Cultural Center Museum, Albuquerque, New Mexico; The Goebel Pottery Museum in Rodental, West Germany; and Southern Alleghenies Museum of Art, Loretto, Pennsylvania.

My work can be identified by my signature and date on each piece. It is satisfying to know that my work is appreciated by many so I have tried to keep tract of where my pottery has gone. I love to do this kind of work and be by myself in my own world of my own creations with the help of God and Mother Earth. Seeing them finished is very satisfying.

I am very proud of my heritage and abilities to help keep our Santa Clara Indian cultural arts alive. Not only is our pottery beautiful but this traditional black pottery, along with the red, is becoming more valuable each year and, as many collectors and dealers say, a very good investment.

My children and I have done pottery making and firing demonstrations for groups by appointment and fee agreements. The largest group we ever demonstrated our work for was when my son, Cliff, and I were invited to "America's Reunion" for the 1993 Presidential Inaugural in Washington, D. C.

People may also see us work in my studio except on Sundays. Certain other days I cannot be there because of my turn to stay with my mother. Most days my son Cliff and daughter Susan are at the studio or my husband, Ted, keeps it open when we are not there.

At my Studio and Gallery I sell my pottery, my two son's pottery, my daughter's pottery, my two grandsons' pottery, my mother Margaret Tafoya's pottery, when available, and also some of my sister's and niece's pottery when available.

The arts and crafts shows where I have exhibited my pottery, and some many times, are: The Arts and Crafts Fair in Albuquerque, New Mexico; The Arts and Crafts Fair in Ruidoso, New Mexico; The Art Mart Exhibit in El Paso, Texas; The Eight Northern Pueblos Indian Artist and Craftsman Shows; The S.W.A.I.A. Indian Market at Santa Fe, New Mexico; The Rio Grande Pottery and Sculpture Exposition in Albuquerque, New Mexico; The American Indian Arts Festival in Albuquerque, New Mexico; The Seven Families in Pueblo Pottery at The Maxwell Museum of the University of New Mexico in Albuquerque; The Gallery La Luz Annual Indian Show; The Santa Monica Indian Arts and Crafts Show in Santa Monica, California; The Indian Arts and Crafts Show in Kansas City, Missouri;

The Margaret Tafoya Family Pottery Show at Red Rocks Park Indian Ceremonial Grounds near Gallup, New Mexico; The Dewey-Kofron Gallery Pueblo Pottery Exhibition in Santa Fe, New Mexico; The Heard Museum Show in Phoenix, Arizona; The Margaret Tafoya Family Pottery Show at Gallery 10 in Scottsdale, Arizona; The Margaret Tafoya Family Pottery Show at the Museum of Natural History in Denver, Colorado; At "America's Reunion" for The 1993 Presidential Inaugural in Washington, D. C.; and I was The Guest of Honor at The Eight Northern Pueblos 25th Anniversary Celebration of Their Arts and Crafts Show in 1996.

Personal shows which I have done were at: The Eagle Dancer Gallery, Sedona, Arizona; Billy The Kid Gift Shop in Old Mesilla, Las Cruces, New Mexico; The American Indian Arts Shop, Kansas City, Missouri; Santa Fe East Gallery, Santa Fe, New Mexico; The Graphic Image, Milburn, New Jersey; and Sunbird Gallery, Los Altos, California.

To date, I have received prize money, awards, and ribbons for my pottery at these shows and dates: The Eight Northern Pueblos Arts and Crafts Show, Best in Pottery, 1996, Best in Traditional Pottery, 1996, First Place, 1973 through 1976, 1987, 1988, 1992, 1994, and 1996, Second Place, 1974, 1976 through 1980, 1982, 1988, 1989, and 1996, and Third Place, 1974, 1976, 1988, 1993, and 1994; S.W.A.I.A. Santa Fe Indian Market, First Place, 1975, 1977, 1979, 1983, 1984, 1986, and 1992 through 1996, Second Place, 1975, 1977, 1978, 1983, through 1985, 1988, 1989, 1991 through 1993, and 1995, Third Place, 1975, 1976, 1978 through 1981, 1986, 1989, 1993, 1995, and 1996, Ruth and Sidney Schultz Award, 1984, Honorable Mention, 1987, Best of Division, 1995; Gallup Inter-Tribal Indian Ceremonial, First Place, 1979, 1988, and 1989, Second Place, 1974; Albuquerque Pottery and Sculpture Expo, First Place,

1974; The Gallery La Luz Annual Indian Show, First Place, 1975, and Third Place, 1976; Santa Monica Indian Arts and Crafts Show, Special Award, 1975; The Deer Dancer Show, Second Place & Honorable Mention, 1979, Second Place, 1982; and The New Mexico State Fair, First PLace, 1984.

Articles about me and my pottery have appeared in: "American Indian Art" Magazine; "New Mexico" Magazine; "Arizona Highways" Magazine; "Arizona Living"; Japan Airlines Magazine, "Winds"; "The Santa Fe New Mexican"; "Kansas City Star"; "El Paso Times"; "New York Times"; "Collectors News"; "Seven Families in Pueblo Pottery" Book; "Pueblo Pottery Exhibition" Book by The Dewey Kofron Gallery, Santa Fe, N.M.; "One Space/Three Visions" Book by the Albuquerque, N.M. Museum; A Japanese book, "Spirit No Utsuwa" ("Pottery of the Spirit"); and documentary film, "With Hand and Heart".

I have been asked by pottery collectors and other friends, if I have a book showing how my pottery is made. Many people have seen our homemade book of color photos with short captions under each photo which, somewhat, explains each step of my work. I had this book with me at most of the pottery shows and many interested people asked about a copy of it for themselves. So this is the book people were waiting for.

STEPS IN POTTERY MAKING

Step 1. Digging the clay.

The special clay is found in veins and pits under the surface of the ground in the hills of the Santa Clara Reservation. These veins of clay or clay mines, in different locations known only to the potters, have been used by Santa Clara potters for many more years than our present generations know about.

1. Digging the clay

This clay has a dark, chocolate-like, appearance and is very hard when it is in the ground. Digging it out is very hard work. I did a lot of this work myself with help from my husband and, later, from our sons. Now our sons do all our clay digging. They use crow bars, pick axes, and other sharp metal tools to break away the hard, but precious and beautiful, clay which Mother Earth gives to us.

The clay chunks would be shoveled into buckets as shown in the following photos, then carried to a pickup truck which brings it to our home.

2. Shoveling the clay

3. Bucket of clay

Step 2. Drying and crushing the clay.

The chunks of clay must be dried very well before they can be broken down for soaking and screening. We usually dry our clay by putting a bunch of the chunks on a piece of cloth or small tarp outside in the sun.

The clay becomes a very light brown color when it is dried out. On humid days I am not able to dry the clay in the sun so drying indoors becomes necessary and also a very slow process.

We usually try to have some dry at all times, ready when we need it. We crush the dried chunks with a hammer or a rock that we can pound with. These finer granulates of clay are now much easier to thoroughly soak than the large hard, moist, chunks.

4. Drying the clay

Step 3. Soaking and screening the clay.

Now we soak the crushed dry clay in a tub or large can. We add just enough water to cover the clay and let it soak for a few days before we sift it through a screen. We try to plan this soaking a few days before we actually need it or before I am almost out of working clay.

We must stir the soaking clay at least once a day to help the soaking of any small lumps that may not have dissolved or come apart in the water. After a few days and after feeling of the soupy mixture with my hands to see if most of the clay has dissolved, we can sift it through a fine screen. The screen removes all foreign particles.

After this we must let the screened clay settle so we can skim off most of the water. This may take another day, then the clay must dry to the point where it will stay somewhat together when put in a mushy ball or chunk.

5. Soaking the clay.

6. Screening the clay.

7. Screening the clay.

8. Screening the clay.

Step 4. Getting and screening the sand (volcanic ash.)

Our clay must be mixed with a fine sand to make the pottery strong, hard, and also to give it the smooth glass property. The sand we use is a white powder-like volcanic ash which we find in pits on another reservation, but not in large quantities like the clay.

Since the sand is an additive, we don't need quite as much as the clay, but we try to keep a couple of buckets or a trash can full, ready for use.

The sand should be left in buckets out in the sun to dry so it can be crushed and put through a screen easier. It must be sifted through a very fine mesh screen before we mix it with the soft clay. The screening takes out any large grit or other unwanted material such as, maybe, some small plant root fibers.

Because of using the same kind of sand for many years, I know what it should look and feel like. After it has been put through the screen, it feels smooth in my hands.

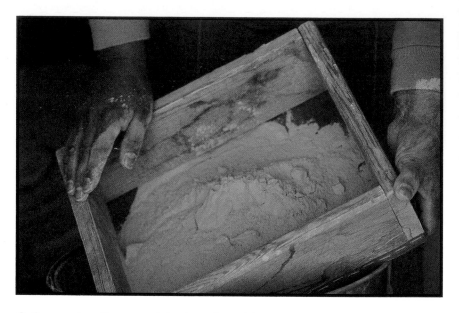

9. Screening the sand (volcanic ash)

10. Screening the sand (volcanic ash)

Step 5. Mixing the clay with sand.

The clay by itself has a very smooth sticky texture. It would be too sticky to work with without some sand in it, besides giving the pottery it's strength.

Since both the clay and the sand have been fine screened, I am able to get a smooth surface on the pottery using this mixture. We mix the two on a cloth or tarp, using only a small estimated amount of sand, at first, compared to the amount of clay. We start folding the sand into the clay with our hands but we do most of the mixing with our feet since we have more strength in our feet using our weight and our feet do not tire as easily as our hands. We may have to add more sand after feeling of the clay to obtain the consistency we want.

The clay and the sand must be very thoroughly mixed to have a consistently smooth clay to work with. My two sons have been doing this clay and sand mixing for many years, so this helps me and it makes working clay for each of us.

I understand that, many years ago, Santa Clara potters used a more coarse sand and more sand than we do today. Some of the clay and sand that was used even had specks of mica in it. These micaceous clay and sand materials made the pottery more durable and waterproof. The surfaces would appear to glitter or sparkle, but because of the amount and coarseness of the sand used, potters were not able to obtain very smooth surfaces. In those days Indian pottery did not have to look nice or be smooth because it was not sold or traded as works of art. It was used daily as utility pottery for cooking, carrying water, for food and feed storage, besides for ceremonial uses.

11. Mixing the clay with sand (volcanic ash)

Step 6. Molding and forming the pottery.

I mold and form the pottery completely by hand using the coil method. I do not use a potter's wheel, and I wouldn't even know how to use one. I have been told that this clay would not work on a wheel. I make my pottery the same way that my mother, my grandmother, and others before them made it, except for my own techniques.

When I want to make a pot, bowl, jar, or vase, I make a ball out of the clay, then I form it into a dish-shaped base on which I can build my pottery piece. (See the following pictures) When I make a very large piece, I use a fired ceramic plate or bowl called a puki to hold the base of the pottery while I build on it.

Now I can add coils of clay to this base, so I roll out some clay ropes of the approximate thickness I want the pottery walls to be. I must make sure I get all the air out that may be trapped in pockets of the clay. These air pockets would cause the pottery to break in the firing.

I add these coils to the base by pinching them together with my fingers, then adding more coils and pinching all of them together. Before I form the pottery up to it's top, I must smooth the inside and outside. I use stones, pieces of wood, tongue depressors, gourd shells, coconut shells, or other shells to do this.

At a certain point I may have to let the pottery set to become more firm so it will not collapse when I add more coils. This depends, of course, on the size and shape of the piece as to how firm it must be. Only experience with different shapes helps me know how firm it needs to be. The shapes that flare in or out a lot must be more firm than others.

I usually decide on the shape or style as I go along building the piece unless it is an order by someone who wants a certain shape, in which case, I must move the clay towards that shape.

I can not always make exactly the shape someone wants. I can only come close. That is why I prefer to do whatever comes out of the clay and whatever I decide as I build the piece.

When I finally get to the finished shape and I have smoothed it inside and out, I let the piece dry for a few days or until it is just moist enough for scraping and carving.

If I am working with another piece and I see that I will not have time to work with this piece before it dries too much, I carefully put it in a plastic bag and tie it shut. This will keep it from drying so fast.

For the traditional shapes such as the ceremonial bowl, wedding vase, water jars, storage jars, etc., I start planning their shapes from the start. For other bowls and variations of shapes, I let my imagination help me to decide what I will create as I build it.

In the days of long ago, when Santa Clara pottery was for utility use, the potters did not worry much about the beauty in shapes, styles, or designs like we do today. I try to keep the traditional shapes and designs, but also, I try to do other things that I like or think are beautiful, or that collectors might like.

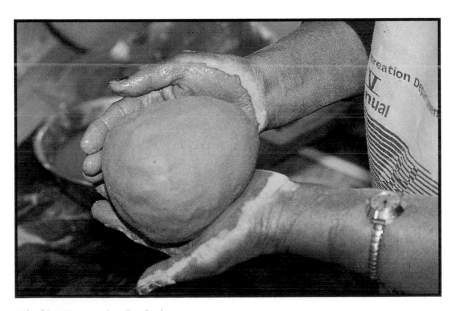

12. Starting a ball of clay

13. Forming the pottery base

14. Rolling out a clay coil

15. Attaching the first coil

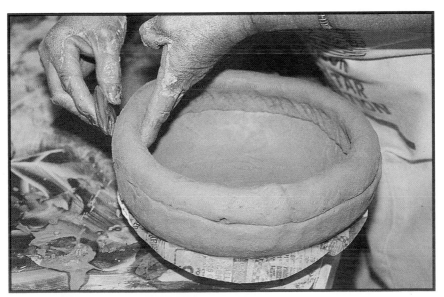

16. Attaching and smoothing the coils

17. Attaching the last coil

18. Pottery building completed

Here are some traditional shapes of our Santa Clara pottery:

Ceremonial bowl—A bowl with kiva steps carved into the top edge, four places evenly spaced, to represent the four directions. In a small hole at the top of each of these four places and with a piece of thread or string, a different colored feather is tied, symbolic of the direction it represents. A white feather represents the snow and cold of the north. A red feather represents the warmth and heat of the south. A bright yellow feather represents the brilliant sunrise in the east, and a blue feather represents the beautiful blue look of the mountains in the west.

The ceremonial bowl is polished on the inside as well as on the outside, since it must hold ceremonial waters when used in our ceremonials.

Wedding vase—A double necked vase with two spouts joined together at the top. This vase was traditionally used in an Indian wedding ceremonial before there was Christianity among the Pueblo Indians. Ceremonial water was put into the vase and, after prayers, the wedding couple drank the ceremonial water. The bride drank out of one spout and the groom drank out of the other. The handle, or connection at the top of the wedding vase, represents the union of the couple in marriage.

Sometimes I put incised bear paws or a carved water serpent on the sides of these vases. (See step 9.)

Water jar (Olla)—A jar with a somewhat smaller neck sometimes fluted up toward the opening. Long ago this was definitely a utility pot for carrying or storing water or other liquids, which were kept cool in the summer when the jar was covered.

I decorate these jars with almost any of the traditional designs, but, most of the time, with the bear paw, water serpent, nature signs, or a rainbow band. (See step 9.)

Storage jar—This is a large diameter jar with it's top curved in to form a flat top with no neck but having a large opening which may have a small lip rising up. The most popular design on these jars is the bear paw but I have done other designs on mine. Of course my storage jars are miniatures in comparison to the ones my mother made. (See step 9.)

The storage jar was used for storing foods and feeds. Baked things like bread would keep from spoiling for many days when stored in one of these jars. The opening would be covered with a heavy towel or such to help keep the temperature and conditions all right inside the jar.

Melon bowl—I usually try to make this bowl as round as a ball, or sometimes somewhat oval, or maybe, sometimes round and squatty like a squash. The melon or squash ribs run vertically all around the bowl with no other added design. This shape is very popular and a style that is very old.

Plate—I make these almost flat and different sizes up to about 14 or 15 inches in diameter. Sometimes I make these more like a dish also. I have a very hard time getting the flat plates through the drying stage without developing cracks or through the firing without breaking. It seems like they must not be made too thin nor too thick and must be supported well while drying. I Thank God and Mother Earth when some do survive.

I usually use the water serpent, bear paw, feather, or sun face designs on the inside of a plate, and I polish both sides. (See step 9.) I am sure that plates like these were very usable in the days when our pottery was made only for utility service. Of course they were not made as beautiful or did not have as much work involved in the carving or polishing. But as useful serving or eating plates, I'm sure they did just fine.

Variable bowls—I make many other different sizes and shapes of bowls to satisfy my imagination. Some may have a shape somewhat like a jar but much more flat or squatty and with larger openings. Some of these bowls may even have short necks or fluted necks with large openings, unlike a jar or vase. I have also made contemporary and modern shapes such as triangular or square openings on bowls.

I use almost any of the traditional designs on my bowls but the one I decide on depends on the shape of the bowl and how the design would fit or look on that shape. (See step 9.) I may decide to leave some bowls plain, polished, but without any design at all.

In the early days these bowls could have been used for serving food, eating, or drinking, since they were made with a more waterproof clay, as I mentioned before, and also polished on the inside.

Thunderbird (Kwa:taa tsire, in Tewa)— Usually after working on some ordinary traditional pottery, and if I have a small amount of clay left from the batch I have been working with, I make a small animal figure or a small thunderbird-shaped bowl. When making these small figures, I use the pinch method, just pinching and squeezing the clay until I form what I want. The thunderbird symbolically represents the forces of nature traveling through the sky in the winds. Symbols of lightening, rain clouds, and rainbows may be included on it to depict storms which the strong winds carry and end with beautiful rainbows after the storms.

Making small animal figures is also how small children learn to make pottery. I started that way, my children started that way, and my grandchildren have been doing the same thing, some of them more advanced than others, though.

Step 7. Packing the clay in the pottery.

About two days after the pottery is made and while the clay is still soft, I use a knife to press the clay in and smooth the surface of the pottery. As we do this packing we look for air pockets and holes which we fill in, using the knife, before we finish by smoothing the surface.

This is an important step because air pockets or holes inside the clay can hold air or moisture which can build up pressure or steam causing the pottery to crack, or even explode, in the firing.

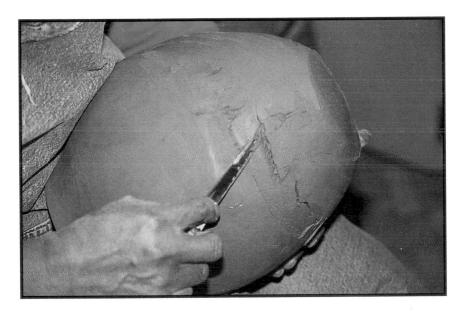

19. Packing the clay in the pottery

Step 8. Scraping the pottery.

While the pottery is still moist but firmly set, I must scrape the surfaces inside and outside with a knife or other tool to smooth out any rough spots. Also I try to scrape away clay from an unbalanced side or bottom to make the piece more symmetrical and level. I even use a carpenter's level on top to check it. I try to scrape away enough to make the walls fairly thin, but not too thin. If the pottery walls are too thick, not all the moisture will dry out and this can cause breakage in the firing. If the walls are too thin, they can crack while drying or in the burnishing process. I can tell by feeling the walls and also by the weight of the piece as to how thick the walls are.

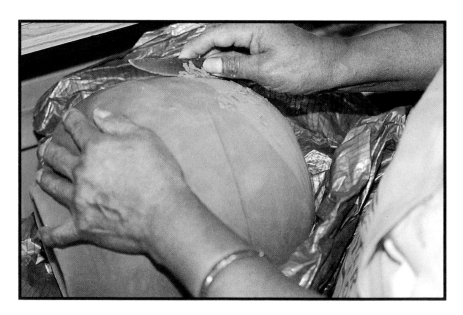

20. Scraping the pottery

21. Leveling the pottery

Step 9. Drawing the designs.

After scraping, I must draw any designs I may want on the pottery so that I can carve out the designs while the piece is still somewhat moist.

I sketch or draw the designs with a plain lead pencil, turning the piece continually to keep the design in a fairly straight line around it.

22. Drawing designs on a large feather jar

I will, now, try to explain the traditional designs I use. I also use my own variations and imaginations on other designs. I have some design names in Tewa, which is our native language.

Here are some traditional designs of our Santa Clara pottery:

Water serpent (Avanyu, in Tewa)—The water serpent design represents various signs of nature such as lightening, clouds, waves, waterways, leaning trees, and mountains. Kiva steps add more significant religious meaning to the complete design.

Bear paw (Kee mang, in Tewa)—This design is the paw and claw prints of the bear. The bear and the path it takes are held in sacred respect by our Indian people.

Nature signs—The various significant signs of nature, such as clouds, wind, water, rainbows, and others, along with the meaningful kiva steps.

Feather (K'ung, in Tewa)—This design signifies the use of feathers in religious ceremonials and dress, showing respect for birds.

Rainbow (Kwa: tebee ba'a) band—This rounded ridge around a water jar looks somewhat like a rainbow, but it also represents the milky way in our galaxy, around the earth.

Step 10. Carving the pottery designs.

Before the pottery is completely dry, I can carve out any designs I have drawn. I do this with wood carving tools, sharp knives, and small screwdrivers. I guess, in the old days, if Indians did any carving at all, they would do it with sharp bones, sticks, and stones. Most old Santa Clara pottery had no carving on it, or had only impressed designs on some. Since pottery was made for utility use back then, designs were not incised.

I have my own style of carving which is very narrow and not too deep, in comparison to other potters. Some people might refer to my carved designs as incised.

After I finish carving on a piece, which could take many hours such as on a serpent design, for an example, I then put it aside for a few days to let it completely dry out. Sometimes I put my pottery in the sun to help it dry out. In drying, the clay shrinks a lot, so this must be considered in the size when making the pottery and also in the design sizes and spaces. Knowing about how much a piece will shrink comes from experience with each different size and shape.

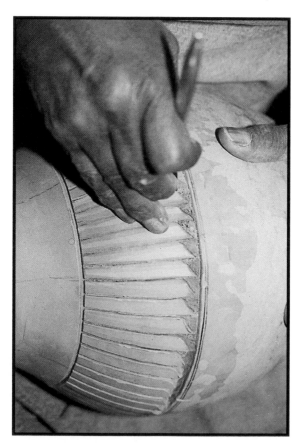

*23.
Carving
the
designs*

Step 11. Sanding the pottery.

After carving and after each piece is thoroughly dry, which is about two weeks from the time I made them, I must now sand them. I start with a coarse grade of sandpaper on large pieces and about a medium grade on smaller ones. This coarse sanding is to remove large bumps and also to help balance the pots more evenly, taking off a lot of clay where it should not be, inside and outside. I must be careful not to chip off my carved edges with this coarse sanding though.

I finish up with a fine grade of sandpaper, including all corners and edges of my carvings. I also sand the bottoms of the pots, setting them on the sandpaper, sliding them back and forth, while turning and tilting them until they look and sit level.

During sanding I inspect the pottery for cracks or holes. Cracks that may have developed during drying and the holes that may have started with air pockets during the building, as I have explained before, will cause the pottery to break in the firing. I have to wipe the surfaces clean of the clay dust in order to see the faults, if there are any.

Of course, now that the pottery is completely dry, I cannot repair a crack or hole, so if I find any, I must destroy or crush the piece so I can resoak and reuse the clay.

It hurts to have to crush and lose a piece with all my efforts up till now, but it hurts even more to lose one in the firing, with more time involved. Also, once a piece is fired and breaks, not even the clay can be salvaged. By working carefully and, with God's help, I hope I will not lose many.

24. Sanding the pottery

Step 12. Washing and painting on the clay slip.

I must wash the pottery with a wet cloth to remove all the clay dust from sanding and somewhat seal off the clay pores on the surface. I use a small brush to wash inside all the carved areas.

Now I can wipe on or paint on the clay slip. I make this slip with another natural clay which we get from a nearby Indian pueblo. I soak this clay in water making it soupy so it can be wiped on the pottery with a cloth or painted on with a brush. This clay is more red than the pottery building clay I use and also this clay slip will smooth out into a nice finish that comes out of the fire a shiny black color which I like. An even brighter red clay is used in the slip if the pottery is to be fired red. I usually have enough of these slips ready to last about a year. I usually paint on many coats of slip with a paint brush. Using the brush keeps my hands clean and ready to use the stones to do the polishing.

The feel of how the stone will slide across the surface and how the shine looks tells me if I have enough slip painted on. The polishing must be done before the slip dries, because the stone would stick and rub off the finish when it is too dry. I learn from experience, how much slip to use and how long it takes to polish an area with a stone.

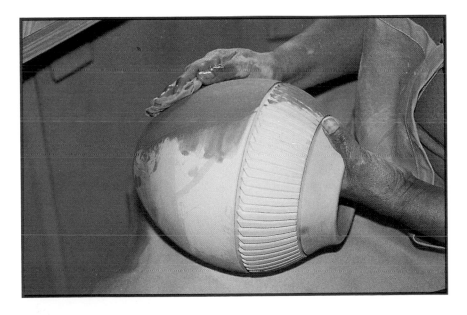

25. Washing the pottery

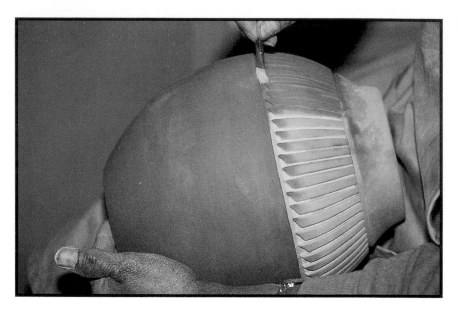

26. Washing the pottery

27. Putting on the clay slip

Step 13. Burnishing.

Burnishing is the polishing of the pottery surface. After painting the red clay slip on the piece, it is polished, tediously, with smooth stones, rubbing over the clay slip until the surface becomes smooth and shiny. I must finish the piece or area which has the damp slip on it before the slip dries because, as I have mentioned before, if it is too dry the stone will scratch off the finish.

I use different sizes and shapes of stones that feel comfortable in my hand and certain shapes to do certain areas. I have my good luck stones which were handed down from my grandmother, SaraFina, to my mother and then, to me. They are fairly large stones with surfaces that can cover larger areas with wide strokes. I also have some medium size stones that are good in most smaller areas or pieces, and some small and pointed stones which I use in very small places, corners of carvings, and such. I bought some of my polishing stones at rock shops. Some of them I have found in dry creek beds and arroyos. The stones wear and become more smooth with use.

The more care and the more rubbing strokes I use in burnishing, the better finish I will have after the pottery is fired, so speed also becomes necessary to do the good job before the slip dries.

I polish only the outside of most of my pieces. However some bowls with wide openings I will polish on the inside, such as ceremonial bowls, thunderbird bowls, fruit bowls, or centerpiece bowls. The polishing or burnishing on the inside does not make the piece completely waterproof or hold water. It only helps for washing with a cloth and soapy water. Water should not be left to set, for hours, in our Santa Clara pottery as it will eventually soak through.

Now, after having completely polished a piece of pottery with the stones, I paint more slip inside all the incised carvings where I want the surface to stay a matte gray after it is fired. I can also paint any other design or feature on the polished surface if I want to and that too will come out a matte gray. I use very small paint brushes to do any finish painting like this. A yucca leaf can be used, and was used by potters before brushes were made.

I must be very careful not to drop any slip on the polished pottery where I do not want it. That would mean I would have to wash the slip off the complete pot or section with a wet cloth and polish it all over again, losing many hours.

I sign and date the bottom of each piece, writing heavily with a pencil, and this will be permanently fired into the pots.

After allowing a few hours for drying of the clay slip finish, like over night, I am then ready to fire these sienna red pieces.

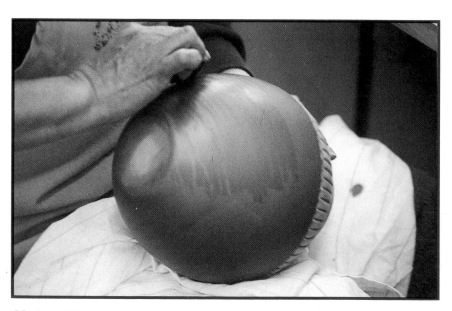

28. Burnishing (Polishing)

29. Burnishing done

Step 14. Firing.

First I must have a calm day with not much wind and not raining or snowing a lot. A shelter built by my husband recently helps a lot so I can fire in some inclement weather. I must build a cedar wood fire on the spot where I want to fire the pottery. Normally, this fire is to dry out the moisture that may have accumulated in the ground since I last fired. Our shelter helps make this less of a problem. We like cedar wood because it burns hot and it burns up completely to ashes.

Moisture rising from the ground during firing can cause stains and even breakage to the pottery. When I cannot see any more moisture or steam rising from the ground, I just let the fire burn down to hot coals. Now I place metal grates, such as milk crates, old refrigerator shelves, or other metal grates over the hot coals, propping them up with tin cans or other metal structures strong enough and large enough to hold whatever pottery pieces I want to fire. A long time ago, before Indian potters had metal grates, I was told, they would build structures around their pottery with buffalo chips or cow chips and wood. Of course they did not worry much about scratches or spots on their pottery in those days when the pieces were for their own utility use only.

Carefully I place my pottery on the metal grate or inside a metal crate, setting them so the polished surfaces will not get scratched or fire marked by the metal. Then I use more grates or sheet metal pieces to separate pottery pieces. I cover over the top of the grates or crate with a metal sheet to keep wood and manure from falling on the pottery. Metal pieces or grates also help to distribute the heat more evenly.

Now, after building up the fire again under the pottery grates with cedar wood, I stack or set on end, pieces or slabs of pine bark all around and on top of the firing grates and metal cover, so that the wood slabs completely cover the firing as much as possible.

The complete enclosure will catch on fire and become a very hot inferno. After a few minutes I must check the pottery to see if it has gotten up to firing temperature. Since the fire is so hot, I must use a long fork to move any of the blazing pieces of bark to make openings where I can see the pottery. The pottery must have a certain pink glow to be at the correct temperature. I have learned from experience just what this glow should look like to obtain the proper temperature. So I keep checking and replacing the burning bark all around the fire until I am satisfied that the pottery is ready.

Now I must cover the entire firing with dry, pulverized,

barnyard manure. This must be done quickly to smother the fire and keep from over-firing the pottery. Over-firing the pottery brings sand particles in the clay to the surface, ruining the smooth black finish. Under-fired pottery does not have the bright black color, but may come out a dull, spotted brown or gray.

The manure must completely cover the top and all around the firing to cut off all oxygen from the outside. This causes the pottery to carbonize and turns it black all through the clay. From experience also, I have found how long to keep the firing covered. Depending on the size of the firing, this could be as long as an hour. If I was firing a piece to come out red, I would take it out of the fire after it had reached the proper temperature, without the manure covering.

After the black pottery firing, I can then remove the manure using a shovel and my hands, scraping together from the top first so that I can salvage the unburned manure for the next firing. The manure on the inside, next to the fire, is burned so I put this on a separate pile where I can soak it with water to put out the smoldering fire in it.

As I uncover the grills and pottery, I must quickly remove the grills with a fork or fireproof gloves to get the hot pottery out.

I use a cotton cloth or fireproof gloves to get hold of the pottery on the inside, if possible, so as not to scratch or mar the outside finish. If a breeze comes up at this time, the fire under the pottery could flare up and the flames that would hit the finished pottery would discolor it so that is why I must remove them as quickly as possible.

Once I have them out of the firing, I place them on a piece of sheet metal on the ground to cool. In the winter, I must take them inside a building as soon as possible because of cold breezes that could come up and cause the hot pottery to crack.

So if the pottery did not break in the fire, or if I did not hear explosions because of air pockets or moisture in the clay and I got them out carefully, without dropping any or any other damage, then I thank God that my firing went well. Losing a piece now and then makes me feel very bad. But getting through a firing without any breakage makes all the sweating over the fire, manure dust and smell, along with all the previous work, worthwhile. A Traditional outdoor Indian pottery firing, like this, without a temperature controlled kiln, has no guarantees but that kind of firing is what makes the pottery authentic traditional Santa Clara Pueblo pottery.

30. Starting the fire

31. Placing pottery in position for firing

32. Placing wood slabs around the pottery

33. Built up fire and checking if pottery is ready

34. Starting to cover the firing with manure

35. More manure covering

36. Stopping the smoke from getting out

37. Completely covered, cutting off oxygen

38. Removing manure after about an hour

39. Removing other covering and pottery

Step 15. Cleaning the finished pottery.

Before I can really tell how the polished finishes turned out after the firing, I must wash and clean the pottery. But I can not do that until I am sure they have cooled off completely. To be sure they have cooled, even on the inside of the clay walls, I usually set them in a safe place overnight, or otherwise I allow at least eight hours cooling before I wash them with warm soapy dish water and a cloth.

I wash them outside and inside where possible, to get out all the soot and manure ash. I do not leave them in the water but I do each piece separately, putting them in to wash, then getting them out immediately and drying them off with a clean cloth.

Now I can inspect the pieces for scratches, cracks, and blemishes. You can see the stone polishing marks through the shine if you look closely, and the coil divisions on the inside are clues to the fact that this pottery is hand made with much work involved.

After about an hour drying I can add any etching that I may want on the pieces, like some animal eyes, teeth, toes, or other details which I did not want carved or incised. I do the etching with a sharp pointed carving knife or tool, or even a large nail.

Seeing my finished pieces, ready for display or sale, makes me feel good with a sense of accomplishment at my own creations.

40. *Me (Toni) and my cleaned new feather jar, outside my studio & gallery, 1994*

41. My newly fired large feather jar received a blue ribbon as shown, at the Eight Northern Indian Pueblos Arts & Crafts Show. (See the following picture)

42. My new large feather jar was purchased by Mr. & Mrs. Walter Gusdorf of Creve Coeur, MO shown here with me in the center, at the August 1994 S.W.A.I.A. Indian Market in Santa Fe, NM where this piece received a blue ribbon. This jar, made earlier that year, also received a blue ribbon at the July, 1994 Eight Northern Indian Pueblos Arts & Crafts Show. Both ribbons are in this picture.

REFERENCES (Chronological listing)

May 31, 1973—"Santa Clara work in Art Mart", article in the *Rio Grande Sun*, Espanola, NM

April 19, 1974—"Quality in Indian arts and crafts", article in *The Sun*, Flagstaff, AZ

April 19, 1974—"The Eagle Dancer", article in *Arizona Living* magazine

April 25, 1974—"Shelton's katchinas featured at Sedona Gallery Showing", article in *Qua'toqti*, Oraibi, AZ

May 9, 1974—"Pueblo pottery evolution traced", article in the *Albuquerque Tribune*, Albuquerque, NM

May 16, 1974—"Maxwell Museum of Anthropology", letter to Tonita Roller from Sally Black of The Univ. of New Mexico, Albuquerque, NM

July 21, 1974—"Viva, San Ildefonso Pueblo", article in *The New Mexican*, Santa Fe, NM

1974—"Art, crafts exhibits", article in the *Albuquerque Tribune*, Albuquerque, NM

1974—"*7 Families in Pueblo Pottery*", book published by Maxwell Museum of Anthropology, The Univ. of New Mexico, Albuquerque, NM

Sept. 28, 1974—"Santa Clara potter to be in Mesilla", article in *The El Paso Herald-Post*, El Paso, TX

Sept. 29, 1974—"Toni Roller to hold show in Mesilla shop", article in *The El Paso Times*, El Paso, TX

Oct. 2, 1974—"Famous Indian potter plans La Mesilla visit", article in *The Las Cruces Sun-News*, Las Cruces, NM

Oct. 4, 1974—"NMSU students and faculty are invited to attend an Indian pottery exhibit at Billy the Kid Gift Shop, located on the plaza in Old Mesilla, Oct. 5-6", article in *The Round Up* student newspaper of N. M. State Univ., Las Cruces, NM

Oct. 13, 1974—"Traditional manner of Indian pottery making still flourishes", article in *The Las Cruces Sun-News,* Las Cruces, NM

Nov. 20, 1974—"Pottery demonstration Dec. 6-7", article in *The Johnson County Sun,* Johnson county, KS

Nov. 24, 1974—"American Indian art", ad in *The Kansas City Star,* Kansas City, MO

Dec. 1, 1974—"Art/Music-Pottery", article in *The Kansas City Star,* Kansas City, MO

Dec. 5, 1974—"Indian Pottery", article in *The Squire,* Johnson county, KS

Dec. 7, 1974—"Potter shows age-old art", article in *The Kansas City Times,* Kansas City, MO

May 6, 1975—"K & L Publications, Shawnee Mission, KS", letter to Mrs. Louise Schaub-Witt from Goebel-Porzellanfabrik, Rodental, West Germany

Sept. 14, 1975—"Tonita Green Leaves Tafoya Roller", article in *The New Mexican,* Santa Fe, NM

Nov. 8, 1975—"Art exhibits, demonstrations seen around E. P., Mesilla", article in *The El Paso Herald-Post,* El Paso, TX

Nov. 15, 1975—"Potter, sandpainter show work in Mesilla", article in *The Las Cruces Sun-News,* Las Cruces, NM

Aug. 14, 1977—"Tafoya family to exhibit at market", article in The Indian Market section of *The New Mexican,* Santa Fe, NM

Oct. 2, 1977—"Pueblo pottery show-exhibition", ad in *The New Mexican,* Santa Fe, NM

Sept. 24, 1985—"Toni Roller interview", on KDKA-TV, Ch 2, Pittsburg, PA

1986—*Margaret Tafoya, a Tewa potter's heritage and legacy*, book by Mary Ellen and Laurence R. Blair

1986—"With hand and heart", 28 minute documentary VCR color film by Otero Savings and Loan Association, Colorado Springs, CO

July 22, 1990—"Places and faces", article in *The New Mexican*, Santa Fe, NM

1990—"Toni M. Roller", article in *The Traveler's Guide to American Crafts West of the Mississippi* by Suzanne Carmichael, Dutton, New York, NY

Nov. 9, 1990—"Artist profile, the Roller family, Santa Clara potters", article in The American Indian Art-Festival & Market brochure, American Indian Arts Council, Inc., Dallas, TX

1991—"Tafoya Santa Clara", article in *Indian Market Magazine*, SWAIA, Santa Fe, NM

Jan. 1992—"Toni & Cliff Roller pottery", article in *Winds*, Japan Airlines magazine printed in Japan INT

1992—"Tewa Thoughts & Expression", brochure by Pojoaque Pueblo Poeh Center, Pojoaque, NM and The Museum of Indian Arts & Culture, Santa Fe, NM

1992—"From the land of Pueblo Indian", writings in the Japanese book, Spirit No Utsuwa (Pottery of the spirit), by Itsuko Tokui, Tokyo, Japan

Jan. 17-18, 1993—"Traditional arts workshop", listing in America's Reunion on The Mall brochure by the Presidential Inaugural Commit-tee, Peake Printers, Inc.

Aug. 1993—"At home with the clay: Pots of tradition, the Tafoya-Roller family", article in *The Santa Fe Reporter*, Artists of the Sun, Santa Fe, NM

Aug. 1993—"Tafoya family hosts exhibit of their entire talented clan", article in *The New Mexican*, Santa Fe, NM

Aug. 26, 1993—"Four generations", article in *The Rio Grande Sun*, Northern Arts, Espanola, NM

Mar. 1994—"Pueblo pottery: Renaissance of an ancient art", article in *Sunset Magazine*, Sunset Pub. Corp., Menlo Park, CA

July 7, 1994—"Valley potters, weavers in Smithsonian Festival", article in *The Rio Grande Sun*, Northern Arts, Espanola, NM

July 1994—"Participants in the 1994 Festival of American Folklife", crafts listing in The 1994 Festival of American Folklife publication of Smithsonian Institution, Washington, DC

July 31, 1994—"Local potter invited to Smithsonian", article in *The New Mexican*, Santa Fe, NM

Aug. 18, 1994—"Of earth and fire", article in The Journal North Indian market 1994, *Albuquerque Journal*, Albuquerque, NM

Aug. 25, 1994—"Two generations", article in *The Rio Grande Sun*, Northern Arts, Espanola, NM

Aug. 1994—"Some artists welcome visitors", article in *The Santa Fe Reporter*, Artists of the Sun, Santa Fe, NM

(Autumn) 1994—"Rattlesnake & Star", ad in *American Indian Art* magazine, Scottsdale, AZ

(Spring) 1995—"Speaks of the earth", ad in *American Indian Art* magazine, Scottsdale, AZ

May/June, 1995—"Santa Fe's native heart", article in *Endless Vacation*, an RCI publication, Indianapolis, IN

Aug. 1995—"Telling the stories", article in Artists of the sun, *Santa Fe Reporter*, Santa Fe, NM

(Autumn) 1995—"Rattlesnake & Star", ad in *American Indian Art* magazine, Scottsdale, AZ

(Autumn) 1995, 1996, 1997—"Galleries, Toni Roller Indian Pottery Studio and Gallery, Espanola, NM", articles in *American Indian Art* magazine, Scottsdale, AZ